A Field Guide to Leadership Development
By
Rita Graziano, MA – Executive Coach

This book is designed to give leaders at all levels a series of practical techniques, strategies, and activities they can use in order to develop in 10 Critical Leadership Capabilities.

Many of these 100 activities I have used while coaching leaders and several I have learned from the extraordinary leaders I have had the privilege to work with. And finally, some I have used myself in order to grow as a leader.

Best wishes,

Rita

Rita Graziano, Focused Solutions Group www.focusedsolutionsgroup.com, 2011

The 10 Leadership Capabilities **Page**

Rita Graziano, Focused Solutions Group www.focusedsolutionsgroup.com, 2011

A Field Guide to Leadership Development

STRATEGIC THINKING

Leadership Capabilities related to STRATEGIC THINKING include: Innovation, Initiative, Creativity, Visioning, Research, Analysis, Synthesis, Presenting, Facilitation, Influencing, Prioritization and Conceptualization.

1. **Industry Scan**

   Purpose: This development activity utilizes research, analysis and synthesis skills to understand industry trends and to identify opportunities for industry leadership.

   Activity: Research the following:

   a. What are 2-3 key industry trends that are or will affect your industry? (now and 3-5 years out)

   b. What are the most innovative industry products or services now available to your customers?

   c. Who are the three most important competitors of your company? What distinguishes their products or services?

   d. Create a one page summary of your findings.

   e. Identify opportunities your company could seize now to create leadership in the industry.

   f. How can you promote these opportunities in your company?

2. **Internal Scan**

   Purpose: This development activity utilizes research, analysis and synthesis skills to uncover opportunities for strategic improvement in company performance.

   Activity: Research the following:

   a. What are the 3-5 greatest strengths of your company?

   b. Where are any recurring breakdowns or problems in the organization?

   c. Where are any gaps in performance in relation to customer requirements?

   d. Create a one page summary of your findings.

   e. Identify opportunities your company may seize now to improve company performance.

   f. How can you promote these opportunities in your company?

3. **Performance Data Scan**

   Purpose: This development activity utilizes research, analysis and synthesis skills to aggregate and assess performance data.

   Activity: Analyze the following:

   a. Gather and review some or all of the following company documentation: 10K Report, Annual Report, Revenue and Profit results for the year, Market Share and Stock Trends, Industry Analyst Reports, Employee Engagement and Retention Data, and any additional company performance data available.

Rita Graziano, Focused Solutions Group www.focusedsolutionsgroup.com, 2011

b. What are the key trends or themes emerging from this data?

c. Where are opportunities for improved performance?

d. What risks need to be addressed?

e. What opportunities and/or risks can you address in your role as a leader, and how will you do that?

4. **Action Learning Team**

Purpose: This activity utilizes facilitation, prioritization and conceptualization skills to identify and address an important strategic, cross-functional issue.

Activity: Facilitate the following:

a. Identify a cross-functional team of stakeholders who can affect an improvement, solve a problem, or seize an opportunity in support of the company strategy.

b. Lead the team in a brainstorming session to identify an important issue that if addressed could have significant impact on the success of the organization.

c. Pose the following questions in preparation for the team's work on this issue:

a. If we weren't constrained by current structure or process and could "start from scratch" what could we do to increase effectiveness in this area?

b. Who should be a part of the effort to address this issue?

c. How would we measure our success in addressing this issue?

d. Create a project plan to implement the work.

e. At the completion of the project, facilitate an after-action meeting: What did we learn that can be carried forward into other important areas of the company?

5. **Strategic vs. Tactical Journal**

Purpose: This activity utilizes documentation and analysis skills to discern tactical vs. strategic activities.

Activity: Document the following:

a. Write a daily log of your principle activities at work for a minimum of two weeks.

b. Group the activities into categories such as:

1. Tracking/Scheduling/Reporting

2. Problem Resolution/Decision Making

3. Status/Updates

4. Creating/Visioning/Setting Direction

5. Communicating/Aligning people

c: Determine what percent of your time over the two weeks was strategic (long term goals, bigger picture, moving forward/setting direction) vs. tactical (fighting fires, managing tasks, implementing procedures).

6. **Strategic Influence Presentation**

Purpose: This activity utilizes initiative, presentation skills, and influencing to gain agreement to focus on a strategic issue.

Activity: Identify and present the following:

Rita Graziano, Focused Solutions Group www.focusedsolutionsgroup.com, 2011

    a. Identify an opportunity you believe the organization could seize that would have wide-ranging positive impact.

    b. Create a slide deck that includes the following:

        1. Describe the purpose of the presentation as well as the need or gap.

        2. Describe the opportunity.

        3. Tie the opportunity to organization strategy and/or competitive threats or market trends.

        4. Articulate the payoff derived from focusing on this issue.

        5. State your call to action and suggested next steps.

7. Stakeholder Synergy

Purpose: This activity utilizes initiative, research, and analysis to uncover opportunities for strategic synergy with stakeholders.

Activity: Conduct a conversation with key stakeholders, and ask the following questions:

    a. What are the top three projects or initiatives you are pursuing currently?

    b. What if anything is a cause for concern regarding these efforts?

    c. What could I or my team do to support your efforts?

    d. Working together, how could we positively impact company strategy?

8. Visioning

Purpose: This activity utilizes creativity, conceptualization, facilitation, and visioning to develop a future perspective for the group or organization.

Activity: Facilitate a group (direct reports, peers or partners) session to identify a future vision by articulating the following:

    a. Mission

    b. Guiding Principles

    c. Core Competencies

    d. Organization Structure

    e. Environment

    f. Future Challenges

9. Challenging Assumptions

Purpose: This activity utilizes research and innovation to modify a strategy in response to customer needs.

Activity: Identify the following:

    a. Identify three to five assumptions customers make about your company. These could include beliefs about what the organization is capable of doing or not doing, ways in which they can/cannot partner with you, your organization's strengths and weaknesses, as well as what problems you are capable of solving for them.

    b. Survey a few key customers to learn their likes/dislikes regarding your company. Ask the following questions: If we could change one thing about how we partner with you, what would that be?

     c. Identify how the company's strategy could be modified or upgraded to positively impact customer's assumptions about how you can meet their needs.

10. **A Bold Idea**

Purpose: This activity utilizes creativity, innovation, and influencing to uncover an idea that can significantly impact organization success.

Activity: Facilitate a team of direct reports as follows:

     a. Challenge the team to brainstorm "bold" ideas that would take company performance to a new level and support achievement of a key goal.

     b. Choose one high value idea.

     c. Use visual aids and charts to describe the idea.

     d. Assign task teams to research and plan the implementation of the chosen idea.

MANAGING UP

Leadership capabilities related to MANAGING UP include: Influencing, Listening, Probing, Self-Awareness, Presenting, Prioritizing, Research, Synthesis, Analysis, and Organizing Information.

1. **Clarifying Expectations**

Purpose: This activity utilizes listening and probing to clarify important expectations/priorities and to test assumptions about performance requirements.

Activity: Plan a conversation with your boss that includes the following questions:

     a. What are the best ways we can partner for success?

     b. What are three things you most depend upon me for?

     c. What is your boss looking for you to achieve this year?

     d. If my team exceeds performance expectations, what will that look like?

     e. What if anything is a cause of concern regarding our team?

2. **Self-Assessment**

Purpose: This activity utilizes self-awareness and analysis to identify an accurate picture of individual strengths and areas for development.

Activity: Create a summary of your own strengths and development areas.

     a. Gather objective assessment data about your leadership and professional style and attributes. Take advantage of the Myers Briggs, DISC, Social Styles, Hermann Brain Dominance or any of the recognized assessments that provide key insights and increased self-awareness.

     b. Participate in a 360 leadership assessment, followed by conversations with stakeholders to learn how others perceive you.

     c. Actively participate in your own growth and development by creating an Individual Development Plan. Share this with your boss.

3. **Be a Conduit**

Purpose: This activity utilizes facilitation, influencing, and coaching to educate and inform both your direct reports and your boss.

Rita Graziano, Focused Solutions Group www.focusedsolutionsgroup.com, 2011

Activity: Identify opportunities to connect your boss and direct reports as follows:

    a. Consider how your team member's activities directly tie to your boss's key priorities and concerns.

    b. Determine what critical information or ideas team members have that can support your boss's success in his/her role.

    c. Identify opportunities for your boss to attend presentations, meet 1:1, or learn new information from your team members.

    d. Facilitate these opportunities for the purpose of supporting your boss's goals, developing your team members, and keeping your boss up to date on your team's activities.

4. Alignment Conversations

Purpose: This activity utilizes probing, presenting, and influencing to ensure that perceptions are aligned and the relationship with your boss is effective.

Activity: Gain agreement with your boss on the following:

    a. Contract with your boss to have periodic 15 minute check-in conversations devoted exclusively to the effectiveness of your working relationship.

    b. Use the following questions as a consistent foundation for these conversations: How well do you think we are working together? What am I doing specifically that you appreciate? What could I do differently to increase the effectiveness of how we work together?

5. "I" Messages

Purpose: This activity utilizes analysis, listening, and disclosure to communicate important information in response to conflict or tension with your boss.

Activity: Identify opportunities to lessen tensions or resolve conflict with your boss as follows:

    a. Following a difficult interaction, write out an analysis of what happened and note the following: How did you feel at the time? And now? Does your boss know how you feel? What is the negative impact to the organization of this interaction? What would be the payoff to the organization if the negativity was eliminated? What opportunities were lost as a result of the interaction? In retrospect, how would you approach this interaction differently? What request would you like to make of your boss?

    b. Plan a follow-up conversation to address the conflict or tension. Using "I messages", communicate:

        1. Your desire to reduce the tension.

        2. Your willingness to do your part to resolve the conflict.

        3. How you felt in the interaction.

        4. Your request of your boss for next time.

        5. Your commitment to an effective relationship.

 Rita Graziano, Focused Solutions Group www.focusedsolutionsgroup.com, 2011

6. **Context**

   Purpose: This activity utilizes presenting and organizing information effectively and efficiently.

   Activity: Plan an update presentation to your boss as follows:

   a.   Begin your presentation by providing context and a connection to the last update. By connecting this presentation to previous ones, you ensure your boss can quickly see context and continuity.

   b.   Provide context by:

      1.   Reminding your boss where you left off last time.
      2.   Reviewing the objective before getting into what and how.
      3.   Asking if new information or discussions relevant to the topic have occurred since your last update.
      4.   Summarize the options associated with this update.
      5.   Inform your boss what you hope from him/her as a result of this update.

7. **Focus on Strengths**

   Purpose: This activity utilizes listening, probing, self-awareness, and analysis to identify a boss's strengths and to employ strategies for appreciating and leveraging what a boss does well.

   Activity: Practice the following strategies in order to focus on strengths.

   a.   Remember your boss has both strengths and areas for development just as you do.

   b.   Identify what you believe are his/her greatest strengths.

   c.   Focus not on changing your boss, but instead on seeing important strengths that contribute to organization success.

   d.   Identify a strength your boss has that you'd like to develop in yourself. Ask him/her to mentor you in this area.

   e.   Look for opportunities where your boss's strengths can shine by inviting your boss to speak to your team on an area of expertise, by forwarding opportunities for speaking at conferences, or by suggesting he write for a journal on his area of expertise.

8. **Seek Other Mentors**

   Purpose: This activity utilizes self-awareness and influencing to identify mentors outside the reporting relationship.

   Activity: Focus on adjusting expectations of your boss by engaging with others who can help you succeed.

   a.   Many times your boss is not the ideal mentor as it is difficult for the best bosses to manage a combined reporting and mentoring relationship. In tandem with focusing on your boss's strengths, look for other accomplished and expert professionals who can provide you advice and guidance.

b. Identify what you want from a mentor and the outcomes you seek from that relationship.

c. Talk with others in the organization to learn who might be a good match for what you are looking for in a mentor.

d. Consider your boss as a partner in this effort by informing her of the mentor relationship and your desired outcomes. Let your boss know that you will provide updates on how the mentorship is going.

9. **Change the Dialogue**

Purpose: This activity utilizes self-awareness, reflection and listening to change any negative dialogue that may occur between you and your boss.

Activity: Break through negative habits and false assumptions about your relationship with your boss.

a. Give up ascribing motives for your boss's behavior. We really can't entirely know what makes another individual tick. Respond only to what you can see and hear first-hand. Resist discussing with others any conflict or tension with your boss.

b. Remember, from Stephen Covey: *Seek first to understand, then to be understood.* Operating from this principle where your boss is concerned will change for the better how you see him.

c. Avoid giving up on the relationship, even if it is difficult. As soon as you give up you eliminate a host of options for managing the relationship effectively or for making it better.

d. Replace the negative dialogue in your head to avoid a self-fulfilling prophecy. Imagine a better relationship.

10. **Lead**

Purpose: This activity utilizes self-awareness and analysis to ensure that accountability for leadership rests squarely with you.

Activity: Whether you work for the best boss, the worst boss, or someone in between, leading your team is your responsibility. Ensure your relationship with the boss supports your own leadership role.

a. Inform your boss regularly of your team's accomplishments.

b. Offer ideas to your boss on how he/she can specifically enable your team's success.

c. Communicate the strengths and accomplishments of your boss to your team members.

d. Learn from your boss: what leadership capabilities do you want to emulate or avoid?

Rita Graziano, Focused Solutions Group www.focusedsolutionsgroup.com, 2011

Building and Sustaining Relationships

Leadership Capabilities related to BUILDING AND SUSTAINING RELATIONSHIPS include: Listening, Disclosure, Collaboration, Valuing Diversity, Developing Others, Working Across Boundaries, Networking, Building Trust, and Influence.

1. **Practice Listening**

   Purpose: This development activity utilizes listening and attending to hear others and to act on what is heard.

   Activity: Use an upcoming 1:1 or group meeting to do the following:
   a. Commit to listening more acutely to what others say by asking two clarifying questions prior to responding to another's comment. Notice your thoughts and feelings as you practice listening more acutely before speaking.

2. **Practice Disclosure**

   Purpose: This activity increases trust in a relationship by disclosing more about you and/or what's behind your position or response.

   Activity: In a conversation with a key stakeholder, provide them greater understanding of you and your position by stating and expanding on the following: "Let me tell you why I feel strongly about this…", "Here is what I have experienced that leads me to see things this way…", "I know I seem adamant about this --- that is because I have seen…", "I am someone who tends to see details more easily than the big picture…". "I am the sort of person who tends to take some time to think things over before I respond…"

3. **Seek expertise and feedback**

   Purpose: This activity utilizes probing and listening to acknowledge another's expertise and to utilize it to create a better solution and a stronger partnership.

   Activity: When developing a program or project:
   a. Identify one or two stakeholders who have expertise in this area.
   b. Ask for their input, advice and feedback on your work.
   c. Recognize them for their valuable partnership.
   d. Give them public credit for helping to making your project successful.

4. **Make trust deposits**

   Purpose: The purpose of this activity utilizes communication and partnering to build a robust trust account with a stakeholder.

   Activity: Volunteer to help a colleague with a key initiative in which you have experience – Tell them you can see the value of what they are doing and you want to see them be successful.

5. **Share professional currency**

   Purpose: This activity utilizes research to share organization, industry/professional knowledge, or tools that empower a stakeholder in their work.

Rita Graziano, Focused Solutions Group www.focusedsolutionsgroup.com, 2011

Activity: Subscribe to relevant news feeds or websites and routinely forward relevant information, articles, tools to a stakeholder. This will provide them with current knowledge that may be utilized to enhance their work.

6. **Share a cup of coffee**

Purpose: This activity utilizes communication and networking to create informal meeting times to catch up, get better acquainted, and to discover commonalities with a stakeholder.

Activity: Schedule time on your calendar each month to meet for coffee (or other informal venue) with stakeholders with whom you want to deepen your relationship. While already at the site or in the building of a stakeholder, tack on an informal chat time for 20 to 30 minutes.

7. **Establish a Peer Learning Relationship**

Purpose: This activity utilizes working across boundaries, listening and collaboration to establish a cross-boundary peer relationship in order to gain a better understanding of adjacent activities outside your domain.

Activity: Choose a peer who is expert in a field or domain not your own and contract to meet periodically in order to share trends, challenges, opportunities, and current activities in your respective domains. Seek ways for both parties to capitalize on this expanded knowledge.

8. **Volunteer to Present**

Purpose: This activity utilizes presentation skills and professional expertise to offer your knowledge to another's team or group.

Activity: Create a short presentation on a unique area of expertise that you can share with colleagues or stakeholders. Offer to present at a team meeting or professional association that your stakeholders value.

9. **Create informal get-togethers**

Purpose: This activity utilizes networking and communication skills to give a team or group informal time to deepen relationships and increase trust.

Activity: Make a list of informal social events or gatherings that bring people together for fun and relaxed conversation. Give team members a choice which they'd prefer and how often they'd like to see these events occur: Calendar quarterly or half yearly.

10. **Establish Office Hours**

Purpose: This activity utilizes listening and building trust to actualize an open door policy and to be accessible to team members for unscheduled conversations.

Activity: Calendar an hour/week (or more) to be available to team members for unscheduled meetings and conversations.

Rita Graziano, Focused Solutions Group www.focusedsolutionsgroup.com, 2011

Business Acumen

Leadership Capabilities related to BUSINESS ACUMEN include: Customer Focus, Strategic Thinking, Networking, Research, and Professional Expertise.

1. **Develop professional connections**

    Purpose: The purpose of this activity is to widen your network to include a variety of professional contacts and associations.

    Activity: Regularly attend professional, user or industry events and meetings for exposure to trends and thought leadership in your business.

2. **Identify business mentors**

    Purpose: This activity utilizes networking and collaboration to identify and contract with business experts who can provide coaching, advice, expertise and learning in the business.

    Activity: Create a list of areas in which you are seeking increased business acumen. Identify the criteria for choosing a mentor for learning and interview 2-4 potential mentors to determine match. Create a contract with the mentor(s) you choose, including length of relationship, how often to meet, and how to measure success.

3. **Create an industry council**

    Purpose: This activity utilizes professional expertise and collaboration to create a forum in which business leaders with diverse perspectives can come together to share unique knowledge and expertise.

    Activity: Create a council within your company that brings together business experts from a variety of domains to discuss trends and to collaborate in order to identify opportunities for the organization.

4. **Make customer visits**

    Purpose: The purpose of this activity is to get close to the customer in order to deepen understanding of the business from their perspective.

    Activity: Calendar customer visits in order to listen and learn about unmet needs, current challenges and anticipated problems.

5. **Connect with thought leaders**

    Purpose: This activity utilizes listening, customer focus and research to identify and connect with business thought leaders through reading and research, social media, or in-person meetings.

    Activity: Identify the 20 most accomplished leaders in your business worldwide. Determine how you can engage with as many as possible using LinkedIn, Twitter, journals, industry forums, events etc.

6. **Invite customers and suppliers to a business forum**

    Purpose: This activity utilizes customer focus and professional expertise to increase cross-pollination and knowledge of trends through partner presentations and discussion.

Rita Graziano, Focused Solutions Group www.focusedsolutionsgroup.com, 2011

Activity: Create or identify a forum within your company in which customers and suppliers can present or conduct a panel around a critical business topic shared by all.

7. **Attend an industry event with a customer or supplier**

Purpose: This activity utilizes collaboration to establish two-way communication with a key partner in order to learn from their perspective and to share your own.

Activity: Invite a colleague from a partner organization to attend a conference or other industry event with you.

8. **Take advantage of Open Source**

Purpose: This activity utilizes research and professional expertise to identify information, tools and knowledge available through open source channels that can increase business acumen.

Activity: Research Open Source sites and activities relevant to your business and take advantage of this information on an on-going basis.

9. **Attend a refresher course**

Purpose: This activity utilizes networking and research to learn current trends and issues in your business.

Activity: Choose and register for a continuing education course from a recognized university or institution on a critical aspect of your business.

10. **Write a white paper**

Purpose: This activity utilizes writing and competitive knowledge to research, synthesize, and report on key competitive differentiators in your business.

Activity: Research the top 3-5 competitors in your business and identify a clear comparison of their strategies and offerings. Include market share data and customer ratings. Share this white paper within your organization and the industry.

Leading Change

Leadership Capabilities related to LEADING CHANGE include: Communication, Influencing, Project Management, Valuing Diversity, Self-Awareness, and Inspiring and Motivating Others.

1. **Conduct an audit**

Purpose: This activity utilizes assessment, collaboration and project management to learn what is working well and what can be improved in the area you lead.

Activity: Collaborate with direct reports to conduct an audit of processes, tools, and results to determine what is working well and what needs to be upgraded. Involve customers in focus groups and/or surveys.

2. **Create a case for change**

Purpose: This activity utilizes strategic thinking and communication to discover the compelling case for why a change is needed.

 Rita Graziano, Focused Solutions Group www.focusedsolutionsgroup.com, 2011

Activity: Answer three questions: 1) Why is this change a priority right now? 2) What would happen if we didn't change? 3) What will things be like after the change has been made?

3. **Chart personal changes**

    Purpose: This activity utilizes personal experience and self-awareness to review personal and professional changes you have made and the experience of those changes and their impact.

    Activity: Create a timeline of your childhood through today. Mark significant changes on the timeline – personal and professional.

    For each change write beneath it:

    > a. The experience of this change was….
    > b. The impact of this change was…
    > c. My learning about change was…

4. **3 Questions**

    Purpose: This activity utilizes self-awareness to better understand how people initially respond to change.

    Activity: In thinking about an impending change, answer the following questions in order:

    1. Do I want to change?   2. Am I able to change?   3. Where do I begin?

    Remember those you ask to change also ask themselves these three questions, and when asking people to change they need time and information in order to answer each question in the affirmative.

5. **Leveraging Diversity**

    Purpose: This activity utilizes brainstorming, listening and probing to bring together diverse perspectives in order to create a Plan for Change.

    Activity: Calendar a brainstorming session with diverse members of the organization – include those from different domains, regions, ages, etc. Ask this diverse group to brainstorm potential opportunities and risks within a change initiative. (Crowd Sourcing)

6. **Change Stakeholder Map**

    Purpose: This activity utilizes stakeholder analysis to create a clear picture of your stakeholders who will be affected by a change.

    Activity: Take a piece of paper or Word doc and draw a large circle. Think of the circle as the universe of stakeholders who will implement an impending change. Divide the circle as you would a pie with each slice representing a group of stakeholders.

    Around the circle brainstorm and write: what are the key concerns of each stakeholder group?

7. **Change emotions**

    Purpose: This activity utilizes self-awareness and observation to list the many emotions people have when asked to change.

Rita Graziano, Focused Solutions Group www.focusedsolutionsgroup.com, 2011

Activity: First list the emotions you have experienced when you've been asked to change. Then add any additional emotions you've seen in colleagues or others as they faced a change. List as many emotions in the face of change as you can; then read and become familiar with well-known change models such as those of William Bridges and Elizabeth Kubler-Ross. From those readings, add any additional emotions common to change. Consider how you will acknowledge emotions and help others to move to acceptance and commitment.

8. **Change Message**

   Purpose: This activity utilizes communication, presentation and influencing to determine how to create a compelling and inspiring message of change.

   Activity: Draft a message to stakeholders about an upcoming change. Include in the message draft the following: The case for the change, the benefits of the change, a vision of the change and how change success will be measured.

9. **Facilitate a Concerns session**

   Purpose: This activity utilizes facilitation and listening to air concerns of stakeholders about a change.

   Activity: Facilitate a session in which stakeholders are invited to air all of their concerns and challenges related to the change. Your role is to listen, provide clarity, and document these concerns. Set the expectation that future communications will respond to all of the concerns once you have captured and organized them. These concerns can form the basis of FAQs and future communications.

10. **Reimagining Change**

    Purpose: This activity utilizes brainstorming, probing and listening to leverage a change initiative in order to spark innovation.

    Activity: Once there is a shared vision for the change, facilitate a brainstorming session with a group of stakeholders asking the question regarding each dimension of the change: How can we maximize this change to foster innovation – to do things differently/better??

Developing Others

Leadership Capabilities related to DEVELOPING OTHERS include: Self-Development, Listening, Coaching, Feedback, and Recognizing and Rewarding Others.

1. **After-Action Report**

   Purpose: This activity utilizes listening, analysis and coaching to develop a direct report in the ability to debrief what worked/didn't work on a project and to capture learning.

   Activity: Ask a team member to analyze and report on a recent project focusing on what learnings should be carried forward to the next project. Coach and provide feedback on their report.

Rita Graziano, Focused Solutions Group www.focusedsolutionsgroup.com, 2011

2. **Action Learning**

   Purpose: This activity utilizes action learning to foster a learning organization and to develop problem solving, decision-making, and team leadership capabilities within team members.

   Activity: Identify a group of team members for an Action Learning Team. Ask them to research the rules of engagement for an AL Team and to determine an issue or problem they can resolve. Provide coaching and feedback to the team.

3. **Career Path**

   Purpose: This activity utilizes assessment and research to identify for each direct report a proposed career path as well as the competencies and behaviors that support the path identified.

   Activity: Ask each direct report to research potential career paths for themselves in their field by interviewing others, reviewing position descriptions, speaking with HR, and taking an interest assessment. Following their research, ask them to present to you their proposed path. You will then probe for clarity and understanding, offer coaching and mentoring including additional options and suggested strategies for achieving their career goals. Clarify the role each of you will play as the individual moves toward their goals.

4. **Individual Development Plan**

   Purpose: This activity utilizes professional expertise and coaching to identify an Individual Development Plan (IDP) for each direct report in support of their development.

   Activity: Create with your direct report a 12 month IDP that includes: Their strengths, their interests, and the skills and knowledge needed for promotion or lateral movement. Establish together concrete goals (SMART goals) for developing capability in the areas identified. Offer individuals stretch assignments. Ask the direct report to provide you quarterly updates on the IDP.

5. **Listening 1:1**

   Purpose: This activity utilizes listening to provide you with the opportunity to understand the development interests and goals of a direct report.

   Activity: Your role in this 1:1 is to ask questions such as:
   a. What do you like most about your current position?
   b. In what ways would you say your current position takes advantage of your talents?
   c. What are you interested in doing that you aren't able to do in your current position?
   d. In what areas would you like to grow and develop? Why?
   e. What are some elements of your ideal position?

   Your goal is to listen and take notes only and to set the expectation for a follow-up 1:1 when you will provide input and ideas on the answers given.

Rita Graziano, Focused Solutions Group www.focusedsolutionsgroup.com, 2011

6. **Represent the group**

   <u>Purpose</u>: This activity utilizes professional expertise and coaching to identify an opportunity for a team member to represent your group within the organization or industry.

   <u>Activity</u>: Review the calendar for the next 3 to 6 months for the purpose of identifying opportunities for development of direct reports in which someone in your group may participate at a meeting or event. Choose opportunities that both match the team member's expertise and also stretch them beyond their day-to-day activities. Ask them to bring back their learnings.

7. **Innovate**

   <u>Purpose</u>: This activity utilizes creative thinking and brainstorming to challenge a team member or members to grow by innovating around the group's work.

   <u>Activity</u>: Ask a team member or group of team members to innovate in an area where the group is stuck or has fallen behind the competition or perhaps where a recurring problem comes up. Give them some basic factors that enable or inhibit innovation, and ask them to report on their innovative ideas.

8. **Attend senior leader meeting**

   <u>Purpose</u>: This activity utilizes professional expertise and coaching to expose team members to senior executives, to provide context for their work, and to learn more about the decision making process at the senior level.

   <u>Activity</u>: Rotate team member's attendance at senior leader meetings and ask them to report to the rest of the team following the meeting. Provide feedback and perspective on what they learned from the meeting.

9. **Partner Lend-Lease**

   <u>Purpose</u>: This activity utilizes collaboration to foster development in a direct report by giving them the opportunity to work for a partner company for a specific time period.

   <u>Activity</u>: Choose a team member or rotate all team members to work for a time at a partner company to increase their ability to observe acutely, to create greater context for their work, to experience a different work environment, and to bring back improvement ideas to the whole team.

10. **Development Dollars**

    <u>Purpose</u>: This activity utilizes budgeting and industry trends to provide team members an opportunity to take advantage of training relevant to their work.

    <u>Activity</u>: Provide a dollar amount for training, and ask team members to research and propose a training opportunity. This can also be done by providing a "dollar matching" for training --- the company matches the amount the individual pays in order to provide an opportunity to access more pricey learning programs.

Rita Graziano, Focused Solutions Group www.focusedsolutionsgroup.com, 2011

Communication

Leadership Capabilities related to COMMUNICATION include: Presentation Skills, Storytelling, Organizing Information, Stakeholder Analysis, and Inspiring and Motivating Others.

1. **5-slide deck**

Purpose: This activity utilizes presentation and communication skills to create and present a five-slide core deck that can be customized for various audience groups.

Activity: Create a slide deck that provides core information about your group or department. Include the following:

   a. Vision
   b. Mission
   c. Strategy
   d. Guiding Principles
   e. Key Goals

2. **Preview key messaging**

Purpose: This activity utilizes listening to get input from multiple sources before sending out an important communication.

Activity: Identify a small group of respected colleagues who will agree to preview a key message and provide you input and feedback.

3. **Toastmasters**

Purpose: This activity utilizes presentation and communication skills to increase the ability to think on your feet, respond to questions, prepare a compelling presentation and speak with increased confidence.

Activity: Join a Toastmasters group in your company or community.

4. **Write a Blog**

Purpose: This activity utilizes writing and professional expertise to increase writing capability by writing often about something of interest to you.

Activity: Create or contribute to a blog about a professional area of interest. Solicit feedback from trusted advisors on your writing style and topics.

5. **Presentation Skills Coaching**

Purpose: This activity utilizes listening and practice to engage in focused communications skills development through a coach whose expertise is presenting information effectively.

Activity: Identify a coach who can partner with you to both prepare for key presentations and to develop your communications skills at the same time. Interview several coaches and find one who has worked with others in your domain.

6. **Junior Achievement (or similar)**

Purpose: This activity utilizes volunteering and presentation skills to participate in a community activity requiring communication of business concepts to children or teens.

Activity: Volunteer for Junior Achievement or a similar group to take advantage of practicing communication and presenting information in a way that young people can learn.

Rita Graziano, Focused Solutions Group www.focusedsolutionsgroup.com, 2011

7. **Practice three Elements of effective Communication**

Purpose: This activity utilizes communication and listening to practice three keys to communication effectiveness in meetings, conversations, and presentations.

Activity: Take advantage of opportunities to practice these three elements of communication effectiveness:

a. "I" messages, to take ownership for communication. When stating what you believe, feel or think, always use "I" messages such as "I am concerned", "I feel there is another way", or "I have a different view on that."

b. Utilize active listening to ensure you heard the other person correctly. Follow up with questions such as: "In other words, you see a, b and c as the key issues", "If I understood you correctly, you would like to see more of that", or "Let me make sure I understood—you are most concerned about c, is that right?"

c. Use "we" and "us" to practice inclusion. Make statements such as: "It's up to us to hit it out of the park." "We have a unique opportunity here." "We will all benefit from this".

8. **Ask permission to give your two cents**

Purpose: This activity utilizes listening to ensure an appropriate time to communicate your ideas and that you will be heard.

Activity: When you feel it is important to provide input (you have relevant information or perspective that will add value or avoid a problem) but you haven't been invited to give it, ask for permission first.

a. "Would it be helpful to hear my perspective on this?" "I have had some experience in this area---would it help if I shared that?" "I have a few thoughts on this topic---may I share them with you?"

9. **Seek first to understand, then to be understood**

Purpose: This activity utilizes probing and listening to increase your ability to use active listening skills in order to respond appropriately.

Activity: Make it a habit to actively listen by:

a. Asking one or two clarifying questions before providing input.

b. "Act as if" at first even if it feels awkward to ask questions when you believe you know the answers and are anxious to respond. Remember: there is power in listening. Have a few at-the-ready inquiry questions/statements like: "That is interesting. Tell me more." "Can you explain that in more detail? I want to be sure I understand."

These at-the-ready questions allow you to actively listen without feeling the pressure to formulate a detailed question. These questions also provide you with an opportunity to gain more information which may assist you in clarifying and asking follow-on questions.

Rita Graziano, Focused Solutions Group www.focusedsolutionsgroup.com, 2011

10. **Plan for conversations – especially weighty or potentially challenging ones**

Purpose: This activity utilizes planning to prepare carefully for important communications.

Activity: Practice effective communication by answering the following questions:

    a.   What are the key points I want to convey? (no more than three)

    b.   Why is this important? What is at stake?

    c.   What would happen if this conversation didn't take place?

    d.   What might be the other person's viewpoint on this matter?

    e.   What do I specifically want from the other person(s)?

    f.   What is the outcome I want to walk away from the conversation having achieved?

Innovation

Leadership Capabilities associated with Innovation include: Risk Taking, Strategic Thinking, Learning from Failure, Change Leadership, Initiative, Customer Focus, and Problem Resolution.

1. **Practice acute observation**

Purpose: This activity utilizes observation and research to identify innovation opportunities.

Activity: Make a commitment to:

    a.   Observe and research opportunities where the competition may be ahead in terms of serving the customer. How might you create a competitive advantage by thinking creatively?

    b.   Watch for process bottlenecks or de-motivators within your work group. How might you create a new way to approach those?

    c.   Be on the lookout for those things that are "the way we've always done it" that could provide innovation opportunities.

2. **Take a walk**

Purpose: This activity utilizes self-awareness and reflection to build in daily "reflective breaks" in order to gain perspective.

Activity: Research tells us that taking a walk, letting your mind "idle" and being in nature fosters creativity and innovation.

3. **Brainstorm**

Purpose: This activity utilizes idea generation and collaboration to let ideas flow in order to find innovative and creative solutions or opportunities.

Activity: Use brainstorming --- alone or with your team or peers – to uncover ideas previously not considered. Use the rules of brainstorming: No bad ideas, the more ideas the better, no evaluation until brainstorming is complete.

4. **Experiment**

Purpose: This activity utilizes experimentation to prototype new methods or products.

Activity: Choose an idea to try out, experiment, and prototype. Get feedback and capture learning to continue building and expanding on an innovative idea.

Rita Graziano, Focused Solutions Group www.focusedsolutionsgroup.com, 2011

5. **Re-imagine change**

   Purpose: This activity utilizes change leadership to identify innovation opportunities within mandated change.

   Activity: When managing a significant change at work, ask the following:

   a. How can this change be a platform for innovation?

   b. What do we have permission to do differently as a result of the change?

   c. How might we experiment with innovative ways of doing work as a result of this change?

6. **Listen to the rebels**

   Purpose: This activity utilizes probing, listening, and observation to uncover innovative ideas through connecting with those team members who resist the conventional approaches.

   Activity: Make a commitment to interview team members who see things differently - who may have radical or partial ideas for how to do things differently. Really listen and probe deeply to understand the seeds for innovation existing there.

7. **Make mistakes work for you**

   Purpose: This activity analysis to mine mistakes made by you or team members for innovation possibilities.

   Activity: Diagnose mistakes by asking the following:

   Why did it occur? How did it occur? Is there an opportunity to do things differently (better) inherent in the mistake? Does this mistake give us an "excuse" to innovate?

8. **Connect**

   Purpose: This activity utilizes collaboration to connect with others in order to create innovation synergy.

   Activity: Identify co-workers or partners who share a passion for the work that interests you. Create a means for you to meet/discuss/share ideas regularly for the purpose of uncovering innovative ideas.

9. **Cross boundaries**

   Purpose: This activity utilizes collaboration and working across boundaries to reach beyond your area of work to solicit ideas from diverse domains, industries, and fields.

   Activity: Make a commitment to connect with people outside your field of work by networking with others. This will assist you in listening and learning about diverse perspectives, allowing you to draw ideas from vastly different professional areas.

10. **Seek creative environments**

    Purpose: The purpose of this activity is to be exposed to creativity in different forms as an inspiration to innovate.

    Activity: Go to museums, art galleries, performance art, street fairs etc. to participate in creative initiatives and to network with creative people.

 Rita Graziano, Focused Solutions Group www.focusedsolutionsgroup.com, 2011

Customer Focus

The Leadership Capabilities related to CUSTOMER FOCUS include: Business Acumen, Professional Expertise, Research, Innovation, and Leading Change.

1. **Research customer feedback**

   <u>Purpose</u>: This activity utilizes research and listening to hear the voice of the customer through your company's tools and methods of receiving customer feedback.

   <u>Activity</u>: Identify the channels in which customer feedback is gathered and reported and review the data. Determine the top 3 to 5 opportunities to delight the customer.

2. **Tie your work to the customer**

   <u>Purpose</u>: This activity utilizes strategic thinking, customer focus and research to learn as much as possible about each customer or prospect.

   <u>Activity</u>: Research three current customers and three prospective customers. Make a list of their "care-abouts", their perceived risks, opportunities, mission and vision. Consider how the work you do delivers on those customer needs/objectives.

3. **Meet the customer**

   <u>Purpose</u>: This activity utilizes listening, collaboration, and customer focus to hear directly from a customer.

   <u>Activity</u>: Invite a customer to listen in and attend a team meeting. Ask the customer the following questions: "How may we serve you better? "If we could change one thing in how we serve you, what would that be?" "What keeps you as our customer?" "What would provoke you to go to a competitor?"

4. **Who does your customer listen to?**

   <u>Purpose</u>: This activity utilizes research to learn where your customers get key information, who they listen to, what associations they count on etc.

   <u>Activity</u>: Research a key customer to learn how information is channeled to them for decision making and problem resolution. How can you intersect with those channels to learn more about the customer?

5. **Use LinkedIn**

   <u>Purpose</u>: This activity utilizes an online professional network to develop a connection and a window to your key customers.

   <u>Activity</u>: Connect on LinkedIn with customer partners, recommend customer contacts that you work with closely, join groups with your customers, and post updates of interest to your customer.

6. **Schedule mutual shadow days**

   <u>Purpose</u>: This activity utilizes collaboration and professional expertise to share with your customer the experience of working in each other's environments.

   <u>Activity</u>: On a given day, suggest to a key customer that you each shadow the other at work.

 Rita Graziano, Focused Solutions Group www.focusedsolutionsgroup.com, 2011

7. **Make the connection**

   <u>Purpose</u>: This activity utilizes listening, coaching, and customer focus to help you and your team members make the strongest connection between their work and the customer.

   <u>Activity</u>: Ask team members to create a presentation for a customer concerning how and what your team does that directly and positively impacts the customer. Provide coaching to team members in developing this presentation. Also ask team members to look for un-seized opportunities to delight the customer and to propose new ways to serve the customer.

8. **Attend an industry event with a customer**

   <u>Purpose</u>: This activity utilizes collaboration to connect more deeply with your customer by attending an event together.

   <u>Activity</u>: Invite a customer to attend an event with you – discuss what you learned from the activity and mutual interests for the purpose of better understanding customer needs and concerns.

9. **Stay current**

   <u>Purpose</u>: This activity utilizes research and synthesis to stay current regarding your customer.

   <u>Activity</u>: Subscribe to news feeds, blogs, webcasts, and websites from and about your customer.

10. **Ask for a customer visit**

    <u>Purpose</u>: This activity utilizes collaboration and influencing to visit a customer site in order to take a tour and meet customers at their location.

    <u>Activity</u>: When in the area of a customer location while traveling or near your work, request a visit and tour to better understand the customer.

Calendar Management

The Leadership Capability CALENDAR MANAGEMENT is related to: Leading Change, Self-Awareness, Strategic Thinking, Communication, and Organization.

1. **Time journal**

   <u>Purpose</u>: This activity utilizes time management, writing and analysis to track how time is spent on a daily and weekly basis.

   <u>Activity</u>: Choose a notebook or journal and commit to documenting for two to three weeks how your time is spent. Write as you move through the day or at the end of each day. After the time period ends, group your activities and tally the hours spent in each grouping. Using your data, ask and analyze the following questions : How much of the time is "interrupted" time? How much was planned? What percent of the time supports your team's vision and mission? How much time is spent in tactical vs. strategic activities? How many hours/week do you work?

Rita Graziano, Focused Solutions Group www.focusedsolutionsgroup.com, 2011

2. **Calendar analysis**

   <u>Purpose</u>: This activity utilizes analysis, tracking and observation to analyze and re-build your calendar.

   <u>Activity</u>: To analyze your calendar do the following:

   a. List all mandatory meetings that add value such as decision making meetings or critical customer meetings.

   b. Create a list of recurring meetings and other activities that seem to create less or no value and ask yourself:

      1. Is the activity or meeting needed at all?
      2. If needed, do I need to attend or can I designate someone else to attend?
      3. Can this meeting or activity be done less frequently?
      4. Can it be done in a different way that will require less time?

3. **Reasonable hours**

   <u>Purpose</u>: This activity utilizes analysis and tracking to determine the number of hours you believe it is reasonable for you to work and also continue to be productive, healthy, and have life balance.

   <u>Activity</u>: Choose a maximum number of hours you will work and commit to that number for the next week. If you work a full time position choose a number between 40 and 50. Recognize if you are currently working more hours than the maximum number you chose, it may seem impossible to cut back at first. You will also want to brainstorm how you can communicate your new work schedule to stakeholders, what activities can be delegated to team members, and how you can prioritize your work hours in order to maximize their purpose. At the end of the initial three days, analyze the following:

   a. How did you feel?

   b. Were there key activities that had to be put off? What was the consequence?

   c. During hours worked, to what extent did you work on the highest priority activities?

   d. What insights and ideas do you have about managing your time and calendar?

4. **Notebook**

   <u>Purpose</u>: This activity utilizes observation and writing to make use of a notebook to identify opportunities to manage time most efficiently.

   <u>Activity</u>: Choose a notebook that you can use throughout each day. Use the notebook to:

   a. Jot down reminders

   b. Capture ideas

   c. Take notes of conversations

   Before going home at the end of the day, take action with regard to each item by delegating an activity, referring an activity to a more appropriate peer or colleague, handling the activity now, marking your calendar for a time when you will revisit the activity, and/or add an activity to the agenda of an already scheduled meeting. The purpose of the notebook and end-of-day action is to "close the day" with as few loose ends as possible and to hand off as many lower priority items as possible.

Rita Graziano, Focused Solutions Group www.focusedsolutionsgroup.com, 2011

5. **Leadership Theme of the week**

   Purpose: This activity utilizes self-awareness and self-development to map your daily calendar to key leadership capabilities.

   Activity: Choose a key leadership capability - one that you want to develop, or is of particular priority, or that is a strength for you - and make it the theme for your work week. For example, if "Inspiring & Motivating Others" is a key capability that you want to develop/practice, scan your calendar for opportunities to practice that capability. Identify several opportunities for that week, and actively employ that capability.

6. **Indicators of an over-scheduled calendar**

   Purpose: This activity utilizes analysis to make a list of indicators that your calendar is over-scheduled and "managing you" rather than you managing it.

   Activity: Create a list of indicators that demonstrate to you that you have lost control of your calendar. The list may include the following:

   a.   Others are scheduling meetings on your calendar without consulting you or without understanding your priorities.
   b.   There is literally no "white space" on your calendar
   c.   You are eating (breakfast, lunch or dinner!) at your desk or during meetings more often than not.
   d.   You have commitments on your calendar for 10-12 hours each day.
        Identify what changes you will make to manage your calendar more effectively.

7. **Multi-tasking myth**

   Purpose: This task activity utilizes research to clarify the reality of multi-tasking.

   Activity: Research tells us that multi-tasking is a myth – the human brain cannot focus on two things at once but because our brains can switch very quickly between items, we create the illusion of multi-tasking.

   Research has shown that given an assignment to multi-task and then to do two things sequentially, it takes more than twice as long to try to do it simultaneously as doing it sequentially. Practice focusing on one thing at a time to be most productive.

8. **Probe rather than rescue**

   Purpose: This activity utilizes probing and listening to practice an alternative to "fixing every problem yourself."

   Activity: It is important that leaders remove barriers for team members, but many times leaders jump in and fix problems for team members, rather than catalyzing those individuals to learn to do it themselves. Practice asking at least three questions of a team member looking for help before you jump in to solve their issue, and notice how you can free up your time for key priorities. These questions might be: "Tell me where you are stuck in finding a best solution?", "What have you tried already?", "If I weren't available, what would you do on your own to resolve this?", "Have you run into this before – and if so, how did you resolve it?"

Rita Graziano, Focused Solutions Group www.focusedsolutionsgroup.com, 2011

9. **Habit 3: Put first things first**

   <u>Purpose:</u> This activity utilizes Habit 3 from *7 Habits of Highly Successful People.*

   <u>Activity:</u>

   Re-read the chapter on "Put First Things First" and ask yourself:

   a. What one thing could I do (that I am not doing now) on a regular basis to make a tremendous positive difference in my business or professional life?

   b. How can I put into practice THE TIME MANAGEMENT MATRIX from *7 Habits*?

10. **Commitment Challenge**

    <u>Purpose:</u> This activity analysis to identify any unhelpful commitments made.

    <u>Activity:</u> Sometimes we make commitments against our better judgment by allowing our arm to be twisted, or we over-estimate our capacity to fulfill each and every commitment. Look at the week ahead as shown on your calendar and highlight any commitments that you made that you: a) are really not appropriate for your role, b) are outside your control or influence, or c) were made to placate someone or to present a "helpful" posture.

    These last commitments are ones which likely should not have been made. One by one, identify how you can renegotiate those commitments and take them off your calendar.

Rita Graziano, Focused Solutions Group www.focusedsolutionsgroup.com, 2011